# CHARM AND STRANGE

# *Charm and Strange*

A collection of poems
by

## LINDA CASEBEER

Adelaide Books
New York / Lisbon
2020

CHARM AND STRANGE
A collection of poems
By Linda Casebeer

Published by Adelaide Books, New York / Lisbon
adelaidebooks.org
Editor-in-Chief
Stevan V. Nikolic

For any information, please address Adelaide Books
at info@adelaidebooks.org
or write to:
Adelaide Books
244 Fifth Ave. Suite D27
New York, NY, 10001

ISBN: 978-1-952570-61-2

Printed in the United States of America

*For Ed*

# Contents

# I.  YE GODS AND LITTLE FISHES

*Imagine the weight*


In my dream I am running
from the marauding elephant
of unwritten poems
and unfinished slides
for the client meeting
running with a certain
panic my fraught limbs
moving across the savannah
in the slowest motion
though when I wake
this is not Africa
usually in these dreams
I am running out of time
or into time to catch up
with the departure of a plane
or a train once a city bus
after I had found a room
full of church circle women
my deceased mother forgot
were coming and I was running
to pick up a dozen box lunches
from the center of the city
close to the office
of my father also dead
but not buried in his plot
his cadaver given away

for anatomy lessons
I expected to pick up
his automobile
stolen instead his insurance
company always chasing
rings of car thieves
never just one at a time
while above me an old
department store clock
showed an hour and a half
had passed for the women
waiting for their luncheon
women tearing bandages
from old sheets to send
overseas and I could not
even create a small feast
to scatter loaves and fishes
among them I am still running
down another block
for oysters or crabcakes
running like in the dream
last week late for a train
to New Orleans leaving
in heaven's seven minutes
and I was nowhere
near the station running
as I will next week to catch
what is leaving without me
planes small and huge
headed to other continents

once my father returned
home after flying
on a doubledecker jet
the second level a lounge
with *a piano a real piano*
*imagine the weight of that*
he would say every time
he told the story we wondered
how the plane could lift off
with a piano on board
and speaking of weight
did I forget to mention
in these scenarios
I am left packing baggage
in cumbersome old cases
without wheels or spinners
valises gripped by hand
so I can never run fast
enough to catch up never
run fast enough

*Dreamscape*

I lay down with you beside
the river I lay down with you
beside the river with an infant
between us the one we never
conceived squirming only a little
your body hard as the ground
and warm against my thigh
as if we were only beginning
the conception yet my breasts
were as heavy as melons
the sky was wide and empty
and blue the sleeping baby
a fragrance between us
later when I arose alone
with a glimpse and a memory
of a village through a window
the river was gone the ground
as barren as anywhere in Africa
I had seen a woman selling ice
but had forgotten to buy any
from her to preserve what
was left of a roasted chicken
eaten after the sun had set
but she had disappeared
and the hyenas nowhere
to be found

*The way of happiness*

The year Trump fell in love with Kim Jung Un
and the planet's hyperbolic trajectory tilted
more than a little towards crazy I fell in love
with Asian tree peonies a gift from the gods
the attraction beginning with one plump bud
on a shrub abandoned by the previous owner
when love leaked out of the house into divorce
leaving the sale of the property to us to us
to us in the way of happiness displayed
by the leaf's shape of a hand with a thumb
and three fingers I recognized as a peony
and imagined a pink Sarah Bernhardt double
ruffled fancy peony pronounced pe Oh ny
by my friend Harriet Parham from Virginia
I cut the bud and set it in a clear water glass
a slow opening single petaled bright blossom
my mother would have called *shocking pink*
the outer petals spread wide to yield
a fireworks display of a hundred shredded
white petals a *Bowl of Beauty* the first
in a season when I ordered enough plants
for an entire peony garden an embodiment
of romance and prosperity an omen of good
fortune a happy marriage though how
to assess any marriage by length or breadth
or depth or else by what magnetizes

pulls us together and apart repeating
like the reunion where a woman reflected
on her life as driven by med school
and breast cancer research a thirty year
marriage to a fellow student her husband
now forgetful but *for the most part a good
marriage* then she repeated *a good marriage*
though it had not been her first unqualified
thought from her south Texas zone 9
where peonies require a little extra effort
to flourish without the benefit of a winter chill

*Arbitrage*

Before her lover gave her oranges stuffed
with stolen diamonds innocent Erèndira
had accidentally set fire to the uninsured house
of her grandmother leaving it in ashes
her heartless grandmother would offer Erèndira
as a prostitute insuring magic paid
the claim as they roamed the desert in tents
under the stars until stars became diamonds

before imagination spawned widespread
derivatives and arbitrage that sounded
more elegant than the exploitation itself
only Lloyd's of London issued policies
accepting risk for Betty Grable's legs
Zorina's toes Jimmy Durante's nose
Jose Greco's trousers from splitting
Abbott and Costello from disagreeing

before a medical school accepted the gift
of my insurance underwriting father's body
my mother was promised his ashes at the end
but after his body was placed naked
on a metal table to teach anatomy students
his remains were buried somewhere else
leaving the stars to teach him how arbitrage
and derivatives insured without reserve

*Linda Casebeer*

before our county owed four billion dollars
for sewer repairs the debt was auctioned
and swapped fifteen times until it ballooned
to an unimaginable size through promises
as empty as my father's grave and all
that we cannot be insured against including
the accidental clots in my lover's lungs
derivative of an ordinary surgery

before my lover and I were wed we watched
Erèndira's innocence erode in diamonds
on the silver screen; afterwards I wrote
a simple poem, and my lover recorded
a line overflowing with oranges on the first
page of Erèndira's story, a slim volume

with lavender cover sealing our forever
romance since who could resist such a gift

*Charm and strange*


Broken down it turned out
*charm* paired with *strange*
named for the lifetime
of the K particle strangely
long and *charm* on a whim
they came in twos by three
like *truth and beauty* until
those names were deemed
too sentimental until that pair
was renamed *top and bottom*
along with *up and down*
the lightest of quarks each
fundamental particle unable
to be broken down any further
the way obituaries had the last
word on Richard Taylor
smashing electrons into protons
to reveal what lay within
the heart of all objects
stories in an invented language
quarks themselves named
for a line in *Finnegan's Wake*
*three quarks for Muster Mark*
begins the story anywhere
the year Richard Taylor won
the 1990 Nobel Prize

we had so little time to wonder
about the heart of anything
was it fractional charges
that had brought us together
into the blue house a world
built of children and work
dogs and cats lilies and irises
if anything we might have found
time instead for translations
of Octavio Paz another prize
winner that year literature
over physics since the story
begins anywhere

*Curtains blowing in the wind*


You and I have written fiction Love
together it can be an intimate act
where we said writing in and out
of each other elicited the yin yang
of voices the *he said she said*
but in the year of the unreliable
narrator the question is *who*
*is telling the truth* if there is truth
haven't we known all along
writers are unreliable narrators
and not all crimes are the ones
reported like the trendy *girl*
*gone* missing the story first told
by the adulterous husband
from his point of view also
a suspect but absent a body
did she leave on her own
or is the girlwife framing him
with *he said she said* is either one
telling the truth if there is a truth
to be told or what about the next
story also a *girl* witnessing a murder
from the window of a train begging
the question *when breath ceases*
*does the story matter if it is not*
*murder* is there a story to be untold

was the bedroom window
left open that night or locked
who tossed the single white rose
into the river was it a signature
or was it the return of magic
realism

*My lyric life*


1.


What if by *flower* you mean *peony*
white petals crawling with ants
beat down by April thunderstorms
the old metal stands falling away

and I mean all that blooms in white
round blossoms in our front yard
simple petaled peonies but also
climbing roses opening all the way

to the edges of what could be promised
rose buds the tightly brighter images
of what is to come in full bloom
pollen dusting the blowsy centers

just before the last petals drop
in the mating season mockingbirds
drowning each other out you whistling
at the one perched on the chimney

when I say *fragrance* you hear *breast*
almost obscene the hundreds of light
blossoms and you imagine that many breasts
at once each one larger than your hand

2.


And when I say *home* and mean
our hundred year old brick foursquare
on the corner with these gardens in front
you hear *house* from your own history

a time when your father took in renters
after the divorce a shock to a ten-year-old
during the second World War the house
later given over to the other family

in the background like the man
across the street on the porch swing
of the foreclosed house made of stone
his roots as old as the Rift Valley

enormous wings shedding pale scales
as he listens to our conversations
and to mockingbird songs that belong
to every bird truck and lawnmower

a very old man who finds meaning
in all the plots that have been lost
since the 1909 blueprints for this
*house with stone wall* were made

*Laughing hyenas*


Love the hyenas are laughing
barking and howling
their siren songs luring us
to the savannah where they wait
for our bodies to be laid out
so they can clean our bones
then leave them to bleach
in the sun *heinous* some say
of the hyenas in any case
their plan is simpler than ours
decisions about the ultimate
provisions for our ancient
bodies to lie down at the end
in a bed of lilies made for infidels

if the Paris in us has no place
to be at peace without bombs
or guns how can we find
our way back to the love dogs
that stopped us in our tracks
when we were ignorant
of Sufism we came to it first
by the dogs barking at Rumi
laughing drunk on love
*love dogs give your life to be one*
Love the hyenas are barking

and laughing at the unknowns
that remain which stones
to leave unturned which poems
to keep which to wish away
in the wisp of the dry wind
and the dust of the savannah

*Bleached bones*


You who caress poetry
in a chocolate bass voice
when the deepest darkest
blue fades from your eyes
*what will be left*
only the great gaping blue
hole near a small atoll
the ocean's largest sinkhole
in Belize we believe
when synapses cease
the corpse will be tinged
blue but cutting into the brain
neurons will be as white
as the sunbleached bones
painted by O'Keefe against
*the blue that will always be*
where warming waters
bleach the coral
expelling zooxanthellae
their absence reflected in white
all colors of the spectrum
beyond the great gaping blue
hole near a small atoll
the deepest darkest blue hue
haunted by the sundappled

manta rays swimming
with great gray nurse sharks
not as dark as the their teeth
on the sand collected
by my mother's hand

*Fog*

The interpreter of my dreams professes
his love for me with the last words from his lips
before the lights go out then sleeps curled
around my back one hand cupping a bare breast

a Shakespeare scholar and devoted fan of Jung
professor emeritus of literature popular culture
and horror a reader of a dozen books at once
a writer with dialogue going on in his head

most of the time he listens with morning patience
to my ramblings about disjointed dreamscapes
and tells me all who roam there are my own personae
the one chasing me and the one I am chasing

in the shadow of the moon the moon itself
and all of the others just below the water's surface
I absorb what he says and nod and go on
as if it's enough to have said the dream aloud

until near fatal clots travel to his lungs and fog
descends to obliterate the entire dreamscape
the next morning my throat closes around
a hollowness that takes my breath away

*Symbol*


No *petit oiseau* in the ruckus
drowning out Parker's bird flute
after breakfast on Sunday
the migrating flock sounded
more like Hitchcock's crows
insistent the noise drew me out
caws mixed with musical notes
at the intersection of songbird
and what was harsh and dark
a flash of white wing
a mockingbird imitation
maybe thirty of them perched
in the old mistletoed oak
on the corner across the street
a plywood-shuttered house
darkened by foreclosure
even though it was cold
on the porch and you limped
slidesteps after a deathrattle
crisis following simple surgery
of blood clots migrating
from one knee to both lungs
but I lured you out to witness
a disturbance so striking
the birds soon required
an identity offered up

easily enough by Peterson
as the black silhouettes of *shrikes*
predators that impale their prey
on thorns since they have no talons
only a songbird's delicate feet

*Rose abstract #1*


Arose from a dream to find
clouded rose the last vestiges
of dawn fading in a simple
dissolve of *permanent rose*
a watercolored chasm of day
breaking across this glassy
laky landscape so softly
I shake your shoulder
awake to show you *rose*
and gentled out of a winter
warm fug you quote Yeats
*to the rose upon the rood of time*
rose the flower the color
of rose a rose is a rose stitched
around the pocket of a chenille
bathrobe my mother wore after
surgery removing her uterus
a rose is a rose sacrificial
as the Lenten rose helleborous
blooming upsidedown
its blossom falling forward
like the head of the one
crowned with thorns who rose
against the stone rolled away
by the *Alleluia* myth sung
from hymns long after The Fall

when original sin elicited
the first thorns along the stem
of the rose blooms that morph
to autumn orange rose hips
rose of the full lips rose
of the sentimental aureole
rose flush of the commingled
bodies defined as sublime
undertones of rosegold make
up the face to imitate a blush
high on orgasmic cheekbones
sex through rosecolored
glasses called romance
never was I one to just leave it
there my own lament
different from Iris Dement's
*I think I'll just let the mystery be*
sex or death a rose or a dozen
in a vase a rose blanket covering
the coffin or a single silk rose
left behind by a certain mortician
whenever he removes a body
along with the immortal question
of who painted the rose nude

*Interjections*

From a woman wrapped in the sun
with the new moon of August beneath
her feet *Ye gods and little fishes*
the same from the lips of our mothers
for times like these just imagine
what the crazies can do with a total
solar eclipse that black lunar disk
passing in front of the sun
changing the patterns of constellations
from summer to winter in sudden
darkness black as the sea of tranquility
lava black for three minutes on a hot
midafternoon turned lushly cool
some said the world would end darkly
during the eclipse as the rapture lifted
true believers up to the sky leaving
the rest to be judged by a god
of the oldtime religion leaving us
all to ask *are we more ourselves*
*with each other as moon and sun align*
and *what is the eclipse* but a trinket
an ornament for the firmaments
a fire a flame or a rock solid hologram
and *what if the mythmakers had seen*
*planes fly* or *astronauts walking*
*on the moon* even though conspiracists

report it was all staged would they still
imagine the departure lifting us right out
of our shoes and up to the sky
and yet we ponder NASA assuring us
we may shed our eclipse glasses
to view the moments of total eclipse
with the naked eye just long enough
to exclaim over a gossamer halo
round the moon

# II. THE QUICK AND THE DEAD

In the years it took the story of written language
painted across the Rosetta Stone and papyrus rolls
on the high chandeliered library ceiling
to dull pastel with grime several generations
fought their wars and almost the most famous
local writer wrote *all this happened more or less*
Vonnegut shelved after J Whitcomb Riley
and Tarkington in the Reading Room
the most beautiful room in the library
where countless men with nowhere else to go
spent their days at long tables hunched over
newspapers hung on wooden scrolls from the racks
gray Saturdays one year I sat at their tables
searched periodicals and microfiche not papyrus
for the secret of what moves the stock markets
a question unrelated to any commodity investments
my parents may have made trading paychecks
for coal and wheat and corn to feed the children
those winter days at noon I would cross
the street from the library to the Huddle House
to order buttered raisin toast cut crosswise
and a cup of tea with babysitting money
then return to the Reading Room
obsessed with the paper I hoped would win
second place and a five hundred dollar Eli Lilly
scholarship to study social sciences

since everyone knew first place would be awarded
to the brilliant and proper daughter of the anatomy
professor her oxfords and gait more like his
than the rest of us who wanted to wear high heels
to swing our hips more provocatively
wanted straighter hair to add to the illusion
those secrets of seduction more elusive
than the fluctuations of the stock market
it turned out markets responded simply enough
to world events profits and market cycles
in a time before the basis of finance unraveled
in subprime mortgages and exotic credit swaps
so many years after the scholarships had been awarded
exactly as expected and the lives of the recipients
had unfolded in the world of financial disaster
I read newspaper accounts of plans to remove
gray layers shrouding the painted story of written
language on the ceiling centerpiece for an addition
leading to lawsuits for a fifty million dollar
cost overrun labeled fraud for major voids
in concrete beams and columns of a new foundation
no longer simple granite with limestone exterior
it was around the same time I ran across the obituary
of the anatomy professor's daughter who had fallen
in love with Japan and studied Asian languages
at Harvard until she gave up her dissertation
lightened her hair and moved to Japan to translate
the one novel that would define her life of fifty years
by the raw grit of drugs human anatomy and group sex
in the cult favorite *Almost Transparent Blue*

*Slipping away*


I suppose it was the memory of long buried childhood
summer vacations echoing in my dream last night
from the old mountains of northern Tennessee
we had always thought if we shouted out the window
down into the valley we would hear our voices
come back to us those summers my parents never
wanted to drive farther than across two states
with four of us in the back seats of the seafoam green
Chevrolet station wagon the last seat turned
backwards where I would sit with my sister
less carsick than the others amid smoke midday
heat and winding two lane roads without guardrails
where old cars and trucks had gone over the edge
left to rust forever

that last year of Tennessee vacations while
my mother packed up canned goods and pans
for the cabin she had a phone call from the church
and learned that a pair of teens had been killed
the youngest a red-headed freckled boy David
the first to put his arm around me on a hayride
and his older blonde sister Denise a brilliant
scholarship winner at seventeen who had lost
control of the car and hit a tree at high speed
that was the year I wanted to shout at my father
to stop the car as he maneuvered too fast around

curves I could feel the vehicle swaying closer
to the edge of those twisted mountain roads
more than ever before

it was not so different last night in the dream
I was driving a big boxy automobile and braked
to an abrupt stop on the narrowest verge
leaving the vehicle tilted toward the edge
of a cliff very high above a broad expansive
ethereal land of yellows and yellow greens
and pale greens and moss greens the pastels
from the landscape we had been rendering
that day on sanded paper through shadings
and blending and detailing using the sharp
edge of the chalk for the leaves and blossoms
in the valley of the shadow while the door
to the backseat had flown wide open
I was horrified that the smallest child
had slipped out and disappeared over the edge
without a sound the others screaming at the top
of a mountain so sheer I could not begin
to descend to search for her and I knew
in my whole heart ever after I would never
be able to live within the echo

*Her body was small in the box*


On a ship anchored off Tortola the island
named for turtle doves I watched tenders
in the distance transport tourists back and forth
while I stayed with *Mr. Fox: A Novel* that twisted
and turned in on itself a metafictional plot
of murder and mayhem when the father
who murdered the mother was viewed
by his daughter as *small in his coffin*
this muse brought back to me my own mother
dead these few months not murdered
unless I did kill her by insisting on morphine
for the intensity of her pain

either way at the end her body was delivered
before dawn one Sunday in June to a Deep South
funeral home tastefully set back in time
where cremations were complicated
by the need for signatures from every sibling
as a defense against drama our own family
unpredictable in that way since years before
one sister had hijacked the burial of our brother
the one closest to our mother and the only boy
so we didn't seem to mind that he was her favorite
until he broke her heart the year she said
he drank himself to death

when we discovered we could bury her body
without all siblings signing since a body
could always be exhumed to settle a fight
discussions turned to a sea island cemetery
three states away Spanish moss palmettos
azaleas and a thousand brown live oak leaves
behind a three hundred year old church
the double headstone already engraved
with her name but not the year of her death
and after a couple of gin and tonics
the good sister thought we could kill two
birds with one stone like the aphorisms
so common among our mother's people

we could bury her in the mink stroller
her name embroidered in the lining
of the coat she waited so long to own
but none of us now could imagine wearing
until that night I reread her will
with her request to be cremated
and I felt her claustrophobia punch right
through the lid of any satin lined coffin
we could choose so it came down to the third
girl a notarized signature I finally asked
for and she did offer more out of the shock
of the death itself coming within a day

in what as children we thought was meant
by *the quick and the dead* in the creed

that told us what to believe in
but leaving only my identification
of her body to the mortician he said
he had prepared her in a cardboard
box for cremation and as if she had shrunk
that last day ever she was small in the box

*Impressions*


Even in a photograph on newsprint
the sheen of oil spilling into the Gulf
comes through in swirls of oranges
yellows and blues with the same crude
beauty evoked by my mother's paintings
when she floated oil on water and color
bled at the edges of heavy white paper
where she would pen outlines in sepia ink
as if looking for shapes in clouds
to see what it all added up to
languid women in flowery hats
radishes with delicate roots
or were they protozoa and what
was the point after she lost her formula
for mixing oil with water and left
the city where she had worked for years
with her friend Jo who dealt in geometries
more attractive to the critics of the fifties
than the curves my mother loved
as much as she loved art as redemption
reflected in entries each summer
to the juried ecclesiastical arts show
at the Lutheran church of the red doors
the act of creation one of commiseration
over marriage largely as unhappy
as any of that time my mother an air sign

my father born under a water sign
these days the patterns of oil shifting
with the weather towards coastal white sands
the weight of the oil hanging heavy
across the wings of long legged waders

*Loki*


Others write about deadmen walking
instead I am a walking flower bright
turquoise white and yellow edged
in black geometric patterned silk
a button on strands of colored thread
hooked around my throat I am a flower
walking among roses and drought loving
vinca small white fairy flowers clematis
thickly covering a cement block wall
I am turquoise against Russian blue sage
yellow against Klondike cosmos
thick stemmed and covered with bees
in the gardens planted to replace lawn
I am walking into the seven thirty dash
for work that follows the shortcut
up Woodcrest a narrow road over Red
Mountain and down into Homewood
I am backing the car out of the driveway
as pain shoots through my thigh
the car still moving into a sharper acuity
of what is caught at the hem of my dress
the kind of bee others all day will tell me
never stings boring anyway into my thigh
a red welt forming under patterned silk

*Signs*

My sister faithfully looks for signs from the universe
that would clarify everything if we would only
pay more attention

when her tire was flat she found our dead mother
speaking to her in the Firestone tire store
where our mother would often go to find a mechanic

for her old white Geo Prism but I was not looking for signs
on that quiet day without wind at the end of summer
only a place to set the one person lime green L.L. Bean

kayak into the water for the first time beyond
the seawall a place without glassy zebra mussel
shells that slice into the soles of your feet

a sandy place like where the heron lands at dusk
always alone it was the inlet that seemed safer
than the broad open water in the front of the house

so without instruction or a plan for reading
the currents and only a vague picture in my head
of what paddling should look like

I got into the kayak and lifted the paddle
along the edge with the water coming towards me
and towards the bridge across to Eden

our name for Noble's island with vegetable gardens
and fruit trees like those his father had grown in Michigan
and like his father Noble grows the perfect white peach

this year is the year his wife Thea died
he said he had planted a thick-skinned
variety of tomato so they would not split open

these reveries as I lifted the paddle for one stroke
on each side imitating the stroke I had seen
others use but I was moving against the current

when I resurfaced after the kayak quickly flipped
I found myself sinking as if in quicksand
but it was only mud where an old wooden dock

had stood until one winter after a flood the wood
had begun to rot quicker until some men came
with heavy equipment to pull out pilings float them

away I had forgotten about the mud that Noble often
dredged out and refilled with sand it was into our undredged
mud thick mud I kept sinking until it was chest deep

one Croc gone the other stuck with a suction
so strong I could barely get my foot out
*stuck in the mu*d a sign that was not hard to read

*How to kill a fish*

The light stayed so late a kind of magic
would settle over the pastel cabins on the lake
in the way Lake Woebegon emerged each week
from the radio or how Paul Bunyon's sweetheart
Babe rose up over the land of ten thousand lakes
I remember the dozens of small sunfish
we were destined to catch after my grandfather
baited the hooks each time the fish trailing
behind the boat in a creel he was a patient man
and I know my grandmother's part in scaling
and gutting expertly the simple flour
salt and pepper for pan frying the fish in oil
in a cast iron skillet but I cannot remember
how my grandfather killed the fish
when John and I Google to find humane ways
to kill a fish we find 1) wrap a towel around
the fish and bang its head 2) slice off its head
3) slice through a fin and let it exsanguinate
or 4) put it in a bowl of ice water and freeze it.
as we read through the options a sound pings
in memory from the pungently spiced water
boiling in a speckled enamel pot my mother
used for live crabs from the traps set at the edge
of her sea island the clatter their claws made
that slowly diminished to silence like the last
kernels of corn popping

*Meshekenabek*


When a man drowned in the lake
word spread by text and email and talk
around town as death sometimes does
anonymously at first no one knew
who had drowned on such a beautiful day
redbuds and crabapples in full bloom
four Canadian geese and nine goslings
pecking in the gravel at the cove's edge
window glass in the old boathouse
broken when did that happen
the drowning of a man in the lake
disturbed the resident of forty years
who didn't like to imagine a drowning
in her lake the same waters that touch
swimmers and waders and others

by noon the name and the story began
to unfold the man without a life jacket
drowned falling out of a fishing boat
into the channel one of three fingers
Lake Manitou haunted by Meshekenabek
the evil spirit with the head of a horse
and a yellow-spotted serpent's body
thirty feet long is that what pulled him
from his eighty-three year old friend
who could not save him but then

the man who drowned in the lake
had buried his wife two months before
ushering *suicide* into the conversation
as the sun set and a full moon bounced
its bright path across the waters

*Splatter*


*Blood* mumbled Ed sitting up in bed next to me with all
the lights turned on at 3AM *red blood blood splatter blood
red red loveliness
in the extreme splattered red petals tea rose red Mr. Lincoln
rose above bloodshed the bodies scattered over there on the
floor the clock
stopped at the devil's hour blood bled true red on a green rug in
this room murder by splatter or slashing* and who was I to say

it never happened just because I only dreamed in
black and white but because I was still lost in sleep not
awake enough to care *splatter*
or *slasher* which of the horror film subgenres Ed often
lectured about to his literature classes I was the one
known to sleep through
hail hitting glass and doors above us kicked in that
night I came awake slower into his nightmare of
murder in the rented room

where we had only been asleep a couple of hours
something about the timing of the ferry from
Nantucket then driving until
after midnight from Massachusetts on I-95 to pass
New York City so we would miss commuters in the
morning a midnight decision
to sleep in Newark where my whole body ached

against the hard mattress I saw only green where he
saw splattered red

my head rested on the pillow as I heard his murmurs I floated
back through the helium and hydrogen gases of the Rosette
Nebulae with a hole in its heart to form the rose then I was
backstroking from the Milky Way's unicorn constellation
to the ecclesiastical arts show where my mother's fabric
sculpture entry of Adam and Eve in the garden of
Eden won a prize

I was listening to the discussion of a painting Jesus
in the garden of Gesthemane on the night before his
crucifixion its strong reds
and greens pulling me in while the critics explained
that painting could never win a prize ala color theory's
complements
of red plus green = Christmas too familiar the
frankincense and myrrh of birth and murder

maybe the clock *had* stopped at 3AM fight or flight
with no resurrection in Newark I became aware Ed
had gotten up to pack
the few things we had taken out of the case so
convinced was he that murders had occurred in that
room he wanted to flee since
we found no palpable body to fight just the essence of
the presence of blood stains on the rug and who was I
to say it never happened

*Jehovah's*


witnesses come
come witnesses
where the screen door
lets in the April sun no
hiding behind a teacup
at the kitchen table
no allowing the doorbell
to go unanswered I am
as transparent here
as the pair is apparent
there only a screen
between to reveal
the world turning small
in the elder's being
as she climbs four steps
to the porch ever so
red the beret atop
her grayed head bent
forward over footed cane
dressed in her Saturday
Sabbath best she refuses
a porch seat the chair
rocking empty instead
as she stands still to catch
her breath her breath
her breath itself flittering

into air beyond the white
butterfly's fragile questions
*have you wondered*
*will suffering ever end*
*what hope is there for*
*my dead loved ones*
*will humans eventually*
*destroy the earth*
*Awake! read it with*
*your Bible* she says *this*
*is the way of happiness*
witness who among us
could refuse her offering

# III.  HOOK AND EYE

*Goldfish*


Nothing fancy here no cockatiels
or parrots parakeets or peacocks
piranhas or angelfish no polkadotted
flirty fins swishing around in the water
just ordinary goldfish swimming orange
in circles in small glass bowls
arranged on a table next to a basket
of hollow white Ping-Pong balls
the goldfish toss older than I the idea
a simple ring toss or is it simply about
where life begins just a one-night stand
imitation carnival in dimly lit
school corridors the booths decorated
with balloons and crepe paper streamers
where all the other prizes are stuffed
animals or enchanted junk
the common goldfish holding onto its place
in the universe where cells of a human
embryo splitting past amoeba at some point
pass through a fishlike stage defying
intelligent design whatever is taught here
sooner or later a child will step up
to the booth and win a prize
when the Ping-Pong ball arcs in the air
and lands with a splash in a small bowl
the hollow ball will float above the goldfish

swimming faster not wanting to be caught
in the small green net the fish finally
transferred to a plastic bag
filled with water and closed at the top
with a red rubberband the water
undulating in the child's hands holding
life not wanting ever to let go
oxygen escaping slowly above the water
in my recurrent nightmare I break
the surface gasping for air arms flapping
coughing up water trying to touch
the bottom with my toes

*The red coat*


Once I had been propositioned
on a Louisville street at midnight
everafter I could define myself
as louche a woman appealing
in some way beyond virginity
with a red American Tourister
case and red wool dress coat
fitted and flared buttoned up
under long dark hair on a cold night

An instructor from the college
had offered the ride going north
before Thanksgiving in exchange
for gas money a common enough
transaction until the car took
its sickening turn and veered off
the highway slick with ice
into a snowdrift forcing a late
arrival around midnight

Hoping to find the Greyhound
bus station to continue north
I was dropped off downtown
in front of a respectable building
where a graying businessman
with a bright flash of diamond
on his pinkie finger insistently
asked if I would go to bed
with him in the Brown Hotel

*Hook and eye*


Stifling August heat hung
over the city that night
the others in the house slept
while sweat dripped down
between my breasts
under a thin cotton gown
the sheer curtains unmoved
by humid Midwest air
gently peeling back wallpaper
in the rented brick duplexes
where I grew up
bedrooms and attics hot
basements coolly inhabited
by venomous spiders
we were told to avoid
the brown recluse the black
widow with a red hourglass
the only relief at night
from heat a cot on the front
porch its screen door latch
a simple metal hook and eye
with a pillow and top sheet
from my twin bed I went
down to lie where a slight
coolness seeped from bricks
a little air stirred not a breeze

but enough to sleep
until sometime near dawn
when a deep voice broke in
*well lookie here if it ain't*
*Sleeping Beauty in the flesh*
I froze eyes closed
then a different voice
*just waitin for love's first kiss*
*izznt she?* I could feel them
move in the bushes near
the porch where the slash
of a knife was all it would take
with only a screen between

*Switchboard*

Until we could afford more
we kept ice in a pail and slept
on the floor of a rented mill
house hung clothes on the line
to dry in October's chill
mice came in through holes
so small we could not find
them to plug with rags

the year I carried the first child
I needed the switchboard job
at a southern furniture company
a headset over my ears
more than eight hours a day
when I disconnected
conversations without warning
some were overly kind

red lights blinked and buzzed
more than one at a time each
unnamed hole a number
to memorize and plug with cords
under fluorescent lights
cords would fall into my lap
over a belly growing larger
ganglia forming perfect patterns

for signals that would make
the unnamed knowable
in winter with a company
discount we bought
a spindled cradle just before
the time came to go home
to the mountain to wait
for labor to begin

*Walking with Rachael in Muir Woods*

Hers is the birth year of the dragon
a small white star hides the memory
of her scalp's oldest stitches
but they would not accept the dragon
or the star as her identify before flying
only the missing blue leather booklet
that reappeared at the last minute
to confirm the year of her birth
the shape of her face her two thousand
year old name as old as the redwood
cathedral echoing the same until
the echo itself falls at our feet
into the misted shadowy ferns
discarded plumage of an elegant bird

*The horses of Delacroix*

We had waited for the winter to elapse
before seeking out the Delacroix exhibit

the winter had been one of destruction
pipes bursting brick walls crumbling

snow and ice on the mountains
stranding mothers and their babes

we had waited until early April's trees
bloomed cherry pink and pear white

waited until the overpowering scent
of yellow lilacs seduced us back outside

and into the museum where a white
marble floor reflected the light

from white walls hung temporarily
with the motion and color of the artist

a Romantic known for his passion
but in the midst of Moorish horsemen

and commentary on the fragility
of civilization we found the horses

_Linda Casebeer_

the curvaceous toss of the head
the lifted hoof the twisted musculature

the strength brightly bridled
the saddles covered in stripes

like Neruda's scene stealing horses
bursting forth from a bleak Berlin winter

*The bigtop*


It was just a little circus on the old winter grounds
where zebras and camels had wandered off
once after the last of the corn had been cut

it was our son-in-law the brother of the highwire
artist who led us to the bleachers set under a faded
striped tent staked to solid Midwestern ground

surrounded by fields it was a sultry Saturday
in one hundred degree heat for the pack up
the babies and grab the old ladies 2 o'clock show

when the cadences of the ringmaster's voice
crackled through the microphone as if to awaken
us from a dream where the dead had reappeared

it was just a little circus but the cues were all there
clowns before a sequined girl climbing silks
another ponytailed and swinging on a trapeze

Scandinavian goats leaping up on pails at the turn
of a whip pyramidal gymnasts and the old highwire
artist working without a net only the music in his head

# IV.  ANGELS AND APOCALYPSE

*On the beach*


Everyone who could was driving away
from the cities everyone who could
was driving towards the oceans
and away from what radiated
Phillip Glass played piano for the film score
etudes that repeated unlearned lessons
everyone who could was driving away
from the cities water was everything
a woman POTUS not Hillary
had precipitated the chaos a woman
who wanted to appear tough answered
a simple attack with nuclearity
that night everyone who could was driving
towards the oceans under the stars
that night everyone who could was driving
away from the cities the country had shrunk
somehow the girls were young again
I drove the old blue station wagon that night
everyone who could was driving away
from the cities I drove in a line of cars
until we reached a dead end in the middle
of a congregation sitting in pews
staring straight ahead gently waving fans
from a funeral home to cool the humid air
electricity was gone everyone who could
was driving anywhere to buy gas

knowing we would run out after we had fled
the city I turned the wagon around towards
home and wondered what to do about water
since water was everything we could set out
pans to catch rain the way I had learned
as a child to catch rainwater for rinsing
hair soft and silky but would the first rains
be radioactive we had never stored water
or canned food for emergencies the stores
had closed after their windows were smashed
neon electric no longer mattered batteries
and bottled water gone no medicine the girls
were young and healthy for the moment
but they would need water where were the bomb
shelters the concrete geodesic domes
the soothsayers of the millennium warned
us we would need water when the end came
how could we exist eating handfuls of berries
from nandina bushes bark and root
while we waited for the acorns to fall
from the hundred year old oak
we had only grown ornamentals not
homesteaders we had no guns no way
to fish when floods had forced koi
from their ponds in the Botanical Gardens
the koi had floated away downstream
nets had to be set as traps we could walk
the few miles there and find a way to net
the koi but the girls would argue
they should not be killed on this earth

where radioactivity was set to spread
until skin burned where was the cyanide
to alleviate suffering the way the etudes
repeated everyone who could was running
frantic for more in the dream water
was everything and the girls were young
again

*My mother dreamed in Technicolor*


The same parade was going by
down Main Street as the brass
band played Alexander's
Ragtime Band *Come on along*

streamers from the handlebars
of bicycles and crepe paper
woven between the spokes
of the wheels it was the strangest

thing the details were so clear
but everything was out of whack
no one was riding those bicycles
that moved along on their own

all of you were young again
riding in the backseat
of the gray Plymouth
your father was alive

he was driving near the end
of the parade no one knew
when the parade had started
sometime after the explosion

all knew it was not a shooting
star or a plane falling out
of the sky the explosion
was atomic the bomb we always

knew they would drop again
what would we do how would
we eat we didn't grow food
anymore no rhubarb tomatoes

peas to shell how would we eat
you were all so young
even your dead brother
came along for the ride

*Strange angels*


*American Horror Story* haunted an old
house a gorgeous Tudor with Tiffany
fixtures transforming light
into ordinary horror not so terrifying
until the second season when the *Story*
took up residence in an asylum
also not so frightening for most
not any more than a haunted house
but it was the asylum of my nightmares
where three strange angels knock
on the door while D.H. Lawrence shakes
his fist at me and shouts *admit them*
*admit them* and when I do
open the door I find Norma
splintered in a Picasso portrait
with her blond son Norman
the father of my children
holding the hand of the third angel
an anonymous towheaded baby girl
wandering off into a clouded dream
without an answer to these questions
1) is it true that angels represent
what has been lost and
2) what am I to do with these three
barefoot angels
that elicit body memories of pregnancy

the little souls moving around in my belly
four times created a certain vulnerability
all hormones and love we were young then
twenty somethings seeking romance
and orgasms playing house and haunted
by Norma who had never agreed
to give up either of her sons to marriage
meanwhile with each birth my focus
turned more inward first in utero
then towards the small warm beings
it was during those baby years
when the last two girls where born
a year apart that I lost track of myself
and world events as they unfolded
a peanut farmer president
hostages taken I think I forgot to vote
the year an actor was elected then later
the Iran contra affair and other whole
blocks of news I never followed
or music that changed with the body
politic all a blur until the marriage
finally shattered after Norma decided
to reclaim her sons and send me
to an asylum *transference* a doctor
would later explain she the strange angel
who would take care of everything
and even when I heard it as crazy talk
I could feel the sensation of walls
closing in of doors slamming shut

gauzy claustrophobia wrapped around
me in Central State Hospital the place
where my own depressed mother
had volunteered as a Gold Lady
and though that asylum has been closed
for many years sensations still
find their way back to me in dream

*Good bones*


Molded of burned lime clay sand gravel
and water mixed into common concrete
a weatherstained slightly cracked angel
gazed up through weeping cherry boughs
overgrown and touching the ground
twenty years after we planted the tree
in honor of spring or love and recorded
the garden's history in disappearing ink
but years later when we wanted to trade
the steepness of Red Mountain for what
was level we found ourselves most attached
to the places where we had removed lawn
to make gardens and of it all the realtor
said the house with gardens would not sell
quickly it was the city after all

Yet two months after the sign went up
we sold the house built by an English
grocer in 1910 over red boulders
too heavy to move sold to a single
woman an attorney who had pulled up
to the front curb in her dark blue
Mercedes convertible drawn to the house
for its foursquare brick stature
good bones as they say and the old wood
inside once painted over with flat black

before being restored she loved the house
but the deal was not without the arguments
of her profession she marked up the sales
contract fought over glasses in the kitchen
cabinet and everything else she could find

Though the angel veiled by cherry boughs
had escaped her notice she also took
possession of it the day of closing
when we left our untidy perennial gardens
originally planted with a design in mind
but grown unto themselves unexpectedly
and we left the angel though the truth is
we had forgotten the barely visible
and in the time since the sale we go back
to drive past the house on Red Mountain
and find the angel has been moved
into the sun on the other side of the red
brick walkway amidst the ever intruding
rudibekia by the woman who lives
in the four bedroom house alone

*Name your poison*


In her hand my neighbor held out a box
offering me nerium oleander a poison
as toxic as the fairy tale's shiny apple
in a kit of age-defying seductions
but what she didn't know is I knew
oleander aka rosebay the bejeweled
clusters of pink or white blossoms lining
my mother's sea-sprayed Carolina yard
with subtropical fragrance the leaves
narrow and willow-like linear lanceolate
oleander the most poisonous of garden
plants in zones 8-10 along the coast
even deer know poison when they find it
planted in a ring around the roses
to be fair I don't think my neighbor *meant*
to poison me since she used the product
herself and it's not the first poison sold
as potion this one a cardiac glycoside
acting on the contractile force of the muscle
of the heart disrupting its function as if any
of us could know exactly how the heart
functions with so many emotions
streaming through its arteries/veins

The main artery in this midwestern town
a mythical Main Street with some storefronts

empty Radio Shack closed also The Times
an old movie theater and up the road
deserted factories never enough jobs
so selling nerium oleander becomes one
in a rat-a-tat tat announcement of a get rich
quick scheme for the price of a sales pitch
oleander with the sound of a round *O*
this is the way a pyramid is formed
by women you know a cousin a friend
a woman at work selling baskets or makeup
or storage containers that burp this time
the reward a Lexus instead of a pink Cadillac
the real money going to the usual suspects
which among them is not an old white man
while in the news on Sunday my neighbor

fainted several times also in the ambulance
as her heart rate slowed to 40 beats a minute
while we who want to understand googled
to find oleander *can* kill but also redemption
for oleander as the official flower of Hiroshima
having been the first to bloom following
the atomic bombing of the city

*Sudden movements*


At midnight when I turned the car
into the driveway facing the lake
headlights caught a hundred geese
huddled at the edge of ice

unsure of what I had seen
I backed up and swung the car
in until lights arced again
across the frozen birdscape

so many wings flapping
and the honking went on for hours
some floated into open waters
others hovered at the edge of the ice

on the night we knew the blizzard
was coming we had not meant
to be here since we had lived
so many years without winter

except for the child without a home
the half grown green-eyed beautiful
blonde child we had known
since she was three years old

it was to offer a home for her
we had bought the house in one hour
of an afternoon on the lake
named Manitou meaning *spirit*

*Whites*


A color or the absence of it all began
with her disappearance and *whites*
what did it mean beyond Sherwin
Williams' 45 exterior/interior whites
in the collection Opaline Divine
Cherish Glimmer Lotus pod Narcissus
Chop sticks Apple slice Fragile beauty
Hyacinth pick one she could have been
any of those or one of the missing girls
on the milk white carton or a girl
with a white hat good fighting evil
in the Saturday matinee westerns
concealed cap pistols galore did she
have a gun or any way to defend her
self whatever *whites* meant it seemed
she was Alice in Wonderland flirting
with a boy the next thing she knew
he had led her down a rabbithole
into the whites of all colors the visible
spectrum reflecting light the washload
of whites separated from colors tumbling
down with her amid the white haired
ancestors' hair uncolored in the genes
of my mother and her mother and hers
*whites* was all we knew of where she
had gone when the judge declared her

a ward of the court and sent her
to w*hites* a bright winter landscape
we would drive through to see her
directed by GPS near Wabash
we found the numbered east and west
roads come together at 00 was it there
that the county boundary began
or ended perfectly flat surveyed in plats
those summer corn and soybean fields
where it turned out Whites formed
around the name of Josiah White
the Quaker railroad entrepreneur
who in the 1800s lost his father
at the age of four he later drafted
and funded a plan for Whites to help
the most deserted of children

*Western Union*

The jig is up when the music stops
playing and it's time to pay the band
or time to pay the bail for the one
calling from jail a bird on the wire
without a get out of jail free card
a young woman claiming to be related
turns out to be only a grifter
Loki the trickster beseeching us
another acts as the police officer
reporting an arrest his voice rushing
through the music of Niagara Falls
on the Canadian side the grifters
are calling from Red Cliff a town
they claim is not visible on most maps
but send the money anyway
by Western Union to a bondsman
and say it's for your uncle your brother
someone you know or it will raise
questions the impersonator says
his shift is almost over and without bail
they transfer prisoners to Toronto
the women's prison where some
of the four thousand are con artists
also the artists whose symbols
connect to our deeper selves
along the heroic journey a call

a dare to possible bliss or fiasco
this is the confidence game to exploit
human cravings greed irresponsibility
honesty compassion what we need
to believe in the kindness of strangers
the hero of a thousand faces
virgin births resurrection from the dead
ancestral offerings sent up in smoke
since we can't take it with us
the jig is up

*The girl*


She has no money she has no wallet
her photo ID stolen she says
she has no driver's license
she has no proof of a marriage license
or the official divorce decree
since her ex husband had a job
she has no Medicaid
she has no food stamps
she has no food
she has no place to live
she has no rent money
she has a social security card
she had a birth certificate
she has an iPhone5 a gift
she has clean drug tests
she has an infant Faith Ann
she has visitation twice a week for an hour
she has to bring her own supplies
but the bag is empty
she has no money for supplies
she has a toothache
but she has no dentist
she has no birth control
she says she could never kill a baby
but her mother once told a judge
she would kill her three stairstep

*Linda Casebeer*

children before she would let them
live with their father the fourth
child she gave up for adoption
the girl has a diagnosis of depression
she has samples of an antidepressant
but she has no prescription to refill
she has a history as a ward of the court
and a runaway
to get money from disability
she claims she cannot get a job
because she is borderline psychotic
the snow is half a foot deep
she has no boots she has no gloves
she has no scarf
she has a hand-me-down denim
jacket with a broken snap at the top
from a grandfather who says
*she is a piece of shit mother*
words that run through her veins
but she has a good heart
she says when she turned eighteen
there were ten different men
on Facebook who invited her to move in
she had an account on Meet Me
where she met her current man
who lives with his parents
she has moved in with them
she has a message on her Facebook
wall written by her ex husband
that says *whore* she has more exes

than she can count
she has a new baby scrapbook
to record memories for her child
she has one trash bag
and a 12 x 12 inch cardboard box
for her possessions she has a fairy tale
her mother told her that a true love
will carry her away and take care of her
and live with her happily ever after
world without end Amen

# V.  DIMENSIONS AND ABSTRACTIONS

*Calculations*


*Shysters* my mother would have called them
deceptive door-to-door roof salesmen
chasing rainbows from one town to the next

they talked fast *insurance will pay for a new
roof all it takes is a few shingles loosened
somewhere we all have them* their patter

of palaces in the sky a conglomerate
bountiful as Pelznickel they would submit
the claim if we would pay the deductible

& sign on the dotted line beyond the reach
of my dead father the underwriter of sky blue
eyes still hovering over the scams that raise

premiums and when we refused to sign
they prophesized roof trouble in the future
casting spells with the words *sooner or*

*later* until water did leak its essence brown
through the white ceiling after four days
of constant downpours we called for a tarp

that true blue icon of water damage
the sign of shingles or tin or tiles lost
in unimaginable dimensions like those

where a child wandered without a roof
over her head at the point when she aged
out of her *ward of the court* status

chose to leave home the same day
she turned 18 and different men invited
her on Facebook to move into the ancient

economic bargain sex for a roof over
her head any man could be *her man*
and I would like to tell you that turned

into a Cinderella story but it has never
been like that for her beyond the blue
where we too would see sky through rafters

after the roof wizard gave us his estimate
the tarp disappeared shingles rained down
from pitchforks at all angles yielding

the original 1910 wooden shakes layered over
four times a fire hazard the wizard figured
removal dollars as the number of layers

times the number of squares plus the weight
of each shingle and the cost of a new layer
of yellow plywood then it began the same

all day pounding as on the roof of the old hotel
in Cusco red tiled headache and nausea of Andean
altitude sickness hammered into the old adage

*climb high sleep low* that led me down through
the cut made by the Urubamba River
into the Sacred Valley that night to sleep

*Forsooth*

In years past when asked to write a story
third graders would pick up a number two
red pencil thick in its lead with no eraser
to print their words on widelined paper
each set of lines separated by one middle
blue dotted line where the vowels touched
they would print their words large since
they had only begun to learn the Palmer
method's Os and loops of cursive writing
before they began to write some would look
upwards for inspiration from the heavens
others would let their heads sink down
onto arms crossed over scarred desks
with defunct inkwells while a few
would line up for the thrill of cranking
the pencil sharpener's handle to peel away
pale wood shavings from lead finally
knowing they could not leave for recess
until they wrote something of their own
each would settle finally into the hush
of a classroom always too warm in winter
the boiler overexpressing heat or nearer
summer the humid heat rising on its own
from the swamp surrounding Round O
South Carolina's early years of school
integration two white teachers sent first
in the year before the busses

As stories were written I would walk among
their desks awaiting requests to spell words
they knew but could not quite sound out
I had listened long enough to their Gullah
inflected patterns the elisions the *uh* vowels
the *scrawberry* for strawberry the *ers* tacked
onto the end of words in the way of Bostonians
I could pick out most of words with little
trouble though once in a while I stumbled
as with sweet Jacqueline eight years old
in 1972 I like to imagine she is a poet
then she was as softspoken and willing
as I was young and inadequate
asking her more than once to repeat
the word she wanted spelled until
finally we came to her phrase *for truth*
the two words lodged in my memory
as I spelled them for her and she wrote
her own exquisite truth it was years later
when I told my husband a Renaissance
scholar the story of Jacqueline's *for truth*
that he caught the origin as *forsooth*
and even then at the time we spoke of it
truth itself was simpler when forsooth
was indeed for truth when alternative
facts were reserved for science fiction

*The swamp*

A two-laned shortcut leading to I-20
took us back into a more intimate time
when Carolina jessamine mounded yellow
blooms over fences at the vernal equinox
their seductive scents camouflaging
the poisons from strychnine alkaloids
the jessamine that was so indigenous
and ubiquitous it was named the official
flower of a state where *carpetbagger*
*Yankee* and *flag of the Confederacy*
regularly erupted in conversations
a place not south enough for magnolias
not quite east enough for Spanish moss
where traffic moved slowly behind
trucks loaded with pine logs cut
from ancient swamps of stagnant waters
the thick trunks chained to the beds
of the trucks that now dogged the narrow
road before us reminding me
of the loggers' children I had taught
in Round O South Carolina when court
ordered integration put white teachers
in black schools before the years of forced
busing as we traveled the light there
seemed to fade into deepening shadows
falling across the patched asphalt

as truck silhouettes took on the shapes
of the righteous self-satisfied Southern
Baptist women who had come calling
to tell me to leave my job at the black school
*Christ the Lord never intended races to mix*
and that school in the swamp was no place
for a nice white married lady and who
was I anyway by my maiden name
if I quit and joined the white columned
church on the square to be saved
I would not go to hell they never did burn
a cross on the lawn though I stayed
for three years until I was pregnant again
and not eligible to teach since the county
considered questions raised by an expanding
belly harmful to children like Cynthia
Frasier wherever she is now
I had wished for her a life not as hard
as her mother's cleaning rooms in the old
motel raising Cynthia and three hellion
brothers on her own always scraping
the bottom of what that low country
would provide her where houses burned
to the ground since the fire department
was so far away they never bothered
to show up the same low country
Kenneth and seven siblings left
motherless after her kidneys failed
the year before the government decided
to fund dialysis when in the fall and spring

humid heat arose from the swamp
around the school without air conditioning
it was easy to claim slavery was gone
until a question was put to the third grade
*what will you be when you grow up*
and in Gullah inflected English *for truth*
from the old English *forsooth* the boys
answered *loggers* and the girls *work*
*at the dress factory* where a bus carried
their mothers to work mornings at 5AM

*Roots*

*Of the three late 2017 UFO sightings*
*in Shelby County, Alabama,*
*"It's not proof of anything, but it strongly*
*indicates that we are not alone*
*and we're regularly being visited,"*
National UFO Reporting Center Director Peter Davenport

Hordes of reporters traveled here and
camped out for a month
not for the sightings of UFOs or of
the Virgin Mary in a cow field

or of extinct birds instead it was a
special election they had come
to cover in this Deep South buckle of
the Bible Belt *Heart of Dixie*

on the license plate as clichéd as *bless your heart* it is a place
where reporters were bound to acquire new myths shrouded

in soft vowels and extra syllables where most wondered first
how to pronounce Alabamian was it **a** long a as in Panamanian

or the short **a** from the state's name tangled in its Choctaw roots
alba of vegetation plus amo for gatherer of turnips parsnips

and Chioggas that grow deep into the religious history
of red clay itself formed from the interactions of

1) climate 2) organisms 3) parent
materials 4) relief and 5) time
once when I was digging up red clay with a mattock to plant

perennials a neighbor asked if we might
could use a few extra plants
from his gray cardboard half egg
carton that held six Klondike

cosmos a gold rush of color named
by priests in mission gardens
for their neatly spaced petals a harmonious whole

he did not tell me they would each grow
to be five feet tall and scatter
gold down the side of Red Mountain those
invasive Mexican immigrants

but reporters had not come to observe the
November dying of giant cosmos
they had come instead to make a digital
collage of a state without polls

ruby red Alabama leaving citizens around the world desperate
to know about crazy were we really crazy enough to vote

for Etowah County's Judge Roy who
would ride up to the courthouse
on his horse Sassy not riding all that well reporters declared

while the judge denied stories of the very young women
he had courted at the local mall calling
them unreliable witnesses

from a long time ago women he had
never met but planned to sue
were we crazy enough to send the Ten Commandments judge

to Washington they made the judge
sounded more mythic than
he actually was meanwhile Ivey a
stout woman-loving woman

who took over when the luv guv was ousted said she believed
the accusers and for a moment I thought
I would have to support

a Republican when she ran again until
she declared bless her heart
and yours she would vote for Judge Roy
since it was more important

to put a Republican in office in Washington there were times
that month when I thought about what
the reporters had been assigned

to do and what I as a transplant had
come to know of Alabama
after twenty-five years that it is hard to
write the truth of this place

some say it's only possible if you were
born here thus reporters called
on Archibald his political column read
aloud weekly in our house

after the election a Pulitzer Prize would
honor Archibald for *lyrical*
*and courageous commentary that is rooted*
*in Alabama but has a national*

*resonance* a most reliable source a
trusted oracle John Archibald
was born in Shelby County Alabama
in a town named Alabaster

after Archibald had pronounced it could
never happen in ruby red
Alabama it would take a miracle that was it as far as it went

for smart election predictions though I
will say reporters had not taken
the time to unearth the miracles reported
in a cow field in Shelby

County the apparitions of the Virgin
Mary or the three late 2017 UFO
sightings in Shelby County first a bright
light visible for a few moments

the second over Alabaster *a bright oval*
*light moving extremely slow*
and a final sighting two weeks before the
election of white cigar-shaped

objects resembling missiles flying parallel
in the sky until they dis
appeared all followed by a different sort
of sighting two months after

the election at the time we had hung
on for hours to the results
from each ruby red county an election
without ever a concession speech

a one-in-a-million sighting in Shelby
County of a rare yellow cardinal
an icon representing Shelby the Senator
not the county for his write-in

vote on an absentee ballot for a prominent
Republican he never named
but had made his vote known to reporters
the weekend before the election

*Legend*


*An owl* shouts one
*it's the middle of the city*
*you're seeing things*
*ready for the loony bin*
persiflage in response
to the outrageous grey
ivory camouflaged bird
almost invisible against
dark tree bark an oak
aged a hundred years

believing or not
they gather at dusk
on the broad front porch
shushing those coming
after the baby points
with one babyfat finger
at a likeness the children
have not seen outside
of zoos or picture books
with *who* sounds

here there a small triangle
the park where people
from three tall buildings
walk their urban dogs

hundreds live near
their vehicles drive past
where carriages are gone
but not hitching posts
and yet what does change
once the owl has found you

*The keening*


As if someone had been lost
the sound mournful and low
from a human it seemed at first
though the source was unclear

several yards touching ours
turned up empty no moans
from injured individuals
so where was it coming from

downtown a railyard whistle
familiar and daily but not
so what a creature's paw
caught in a trap or a tomcat

caterwauling not in daylight
a cote a bevy a dole a dule
a flight so many names
for a group of mourning doves

but none feeding on the ground
only a drab female cardinal
pecking around the hulls
of spent sunflower seeds

as the silence lengthened
I returned inside to the table

to pour over a box of half pastels
sixty colors Rembrandt's

general selection for that day's
lesson in abstraction earlier
Ed had finished his piece
so I was alone as the low wail

began again and I found
myself opening the back door
once more to stand still
and focus on a large dead bough

lodged in a crooked Y leaning
between two old oaks
it could have been the bough
swaying *swing low sweet chariot*

but instead no sound only leaves
in the breeze as the door closed
I returned to blow air gently
across paper to shake away

colored chalk dust and continue
the overlap of pastel polygons
on a black surface until twice
more low moans interrupted

since I had not tried the front
door it could have been

the creak of a swing the girls
had given us two houses ago

except the swing hadn't
been hung yet on the porch
facing the park where once
we had seen an owl at dusk

when I looked out on this day
at midday the sound ceased
again for the moment
the light too harsh

the park as empty
as the spaces where death
settles among us
a mockingbird warbling on

*Direction*

Which way is it really
I have never known
Ed has said to me when
we come out of a hotel
room together *just turn*
*the opposite way of what*
*you think it will be*
but that advice causes
me to pause confused
if only it were that easy
there are nights when
I still wake in a torrid
nightmare the sultry
heat bearing down on
the banks of the Amazon
the Napo rivers where
we had came by boat
from Iquitos no roads in
where expensive rented
rooms were tents
with latrines and advice
to zip boots into duffel
bags at night to avoid
scorpions the world
vertical without a horizon
line the canopy over 100 feet

up and where all paths
looked the same except
to guides who knew paths
like the backs of their hands
guides who would chitter
at a high pitch to the next
one down the line
when they saw a snake
on the path the group
was always in the hands
of guides except for
the way back from
the canopy stairway
where they assumed
we would choose two
turns leading back to camp
but lost in my nightmare
in the primary rain
forest after all I was one
with the rest who threw
coins in the river a wish
to return I again found
a place without landmarks
it could have been only
those two simple turns
back after climbing down
the stairway leading
from the swinging bridges
a fantasy world of birds
their stained glass colors

flashing in the sunlight
at the top of the canopy
a turquoise cotinga
a paradise tanager
parrots and beyond birds
blue morpho butterflies
where pilots flying overhead
had sited a blue so bright
it could leave a retinal
afterimage all darkened
and disappeared down
the stairs where sun
no longer reached
where paths looked all
the same vines wrapping
around strangled fig trees
buttressed roots the devil's
apple poison to the touch
the rainforest home to pythons
and boas and piranha
these last only a symbolic
threat but not scorpions
I awakened my heart racing
with the question *which*
*way is it really*

*Dimensions*

1. Where n=1 height or depth or width but not two of these

2. The trick is to create the illusion of three dimensions
   with paint on a flat canvas where only ever two exist
   together as D.H. Lawrence claimed Cezanne established
   that *matter actually exists* independent of human regard
   by the very *applyness* of the apples he painted
   *succulent cannon balls* said one critic who reviewed
   Cezanne's portraits without praise while the *mort*
   of still life remained as breathless as the Rose Apple
   tree bearing the golden fruit of immortality
   szyigium jambo Myrtaceae words on paper or now
   a screen if not for the Buddha would we even
   be aware of the Rose Apple tree or its relative
   the Blue Lilly Pilly to mention just for the music
   of its name

3. Sculpture adds the third dimension where basswood
   can be turned and turned and turned around
   again to find the answer to the muscle of the horse
   Ira Chaffin taught me to carve before he died
   he knew he would leave behind work
   that would last in the physical world his bronzes
   like the commissioned 7 foot statue of a university
   president on a pedestal in the park the human
   figure designed larger than life to be more pleasing

to the eye and since his death was sudden he also
left my carousel horse legless among the assorted
basswood pieces and parts

4.    What of the fourth dimension the tempo of music
*does time exist* to physicists is entirely the wrong
question *check your watch* they say as they stand
in the shadows of the black holes of our Milky Way

5.    And five, an abstraction of mathematics
where apples glow with cosmic gas as they
along with carousel horses and words alike
are devoured by the enormous black hole
at the very center of the Milky Way in our galaxy
how is it *our* galaxy and how does that deep space
in the collective unconscious belong to us

*The road is closed*


Slants of orange like morning sunlight
cross the white barricades to announce
*the road is closed* and in tones as flat
as Midwestern geography I can tell you
those barricades are solid not mystic
hardly based on syllogisms in Ohio
a name small children like to wrap
their mouths around for its double O's
it comes down to the logistics
of barricaded State Road 168 Geauga
County's project to replace culverts
the road closing clear to all residents
but not to Siri as I ask for directions
she says *go east on state road 168*
with fields all around and skies wide
enough I find east easily by the path
of the sun though from the roundabout
no other roads head east no matter
which town I head for once Aurora OH
two towns over a UPS store for shipping
or Cleveland's renowned gardens
or the gallery and woodworking shop
in Garrettsville no matter the town
it's always the same directive
on leaving Burton a village of pancake
festivals and clear pure maple syrup

tapped from red maples though
I have come here not for tourism
but to have basswood glued up
and cut with a bandsaw into body
parts for carousel animals
I plan to carve so when I do not follow
*go east* Siri's tone becomes a sigh
*proceed to the route* and without a route
I turn north into the unknown
hoping Siri will find and redirect me
past where the road is closed

*The story of life*


We could feel the evening falling around us
though it was noon when clouds covered the sun
above the chapel lit only by natural light
filtering through the windows
and upwards from the window wells
the guidebook said low light lent an ancient
and melancholy air to the fresco we had come
to Italy to see God the father creating Adam
their fingers almost touching except for a small
space left between the two in anticipation
of that moment when God would complete
his creation but in the dull light the fresco
distant and blurred by macular degeneration
and glaucoma for Ed who decided to ask
the guards what time they would turn on
the lights after all in the story of life God
had risen into the sky with arms outstretched
to separate light from darkness evening
and morning of the first day but that day
Ed was one of those the official husher
tried every few minutes to quiet
the crowd forever changing but always
always looking up and sighing

*Life studies*


### Kandinsky at the Guggenheim

Early work the lights of Moscow at night
so many colored oils on white white walls
spiraling upwards towards paramecia
and other early life forms at the end of his life
a retrospective the work of a painter
Ed had seen decades before in Munich
those same years when my girls were young
and learning the names of shells on the beach
from my mother *wentletrap* for spiral staircase
small white treasures plucked with plump hands
from the sands of the tidal pool's spiral ridges
like the structure of the Guggenheim
with waves of color and design washing over
as we climbed higher intensity spilling over
the mountains into numbered improvisations
emerging at the end as biomorphic images
eclipsing a vocabulary of forms where all
of the stories we had told ourselves
all of the models for art we had missed
all of the blocks we had found to creating
paintings and poems fell away in the arc
of a Blaue Reiter painter

*Scattering grand abstractions*


Creating heaven on earth
some say is eschaton
a blissful place in the sun
a place where the news
does not intrude
in the naming of children
or the unveiling of graves
others say eschaton
is the end of the world
good and evil judged
the unknown revealed
the missing plane
murderers confirmed
the mysteries of sex
and birth love and death
unraveled like dropped
stiches of soft yarn
each stitch at the end
a reminiscence
a seduction of another
language past translation
eschaton chosen more for
its sound than its *ism*

# Acknowledgements

"Walking with Rachael in Muir Woods," *California Poetry Society Quarterly,* 2009.

"Goldfish" *The Light in Ordinary Things*, Fearless Books, 2009.

"Switchboard" *The Light in Ordinary Things*, Fearless Books, 2009.

"Fog," *Chest,* 2010.

"Symbol," *Slant,* May, 2010.

"The Anatomy Professor's Daughter," *Slant, 2011.*

" Myth,"/Western Union *Earth's Daughters,* 2012.

"My Lyric Life," *Earth's Daughters,* 2012.

"Arbitrage," *Hospital Drive,* 2012.

"The Big Top," *Earth's Daughters,* 2014.

"How to Kill a Fish" *Third Wednesday,* 2015.

"Impressions," *Soundings,* 2015.

"The Girl," *Circe's Lament,* an anthology, 2015.

"Name Your Poison," *Chest, 2016.*

"Dreamscape" *Pinyon Press* 2016.

"Hook and Eye" *Slant* 2016.

"Loki" *Raven's Perch 2016.*

"Imagine the Weight" *Slant 2018.*

"Good Bones" and "Curtains that Blow in the Wind" forth-coming in *Boned 2019*

"charm and strange," *The Big Picture Review, 2018.*

"Her body is small in the box," "Strange angels," "The story of life," *Adelaide Literary Review, August, 2018.*

"The Keening", *Canary 2019*

"On the Beach" Nominated by Canary for a Pushcart Prize

# About the Author

Tabitha Bates/Woody ONeal (photo)

**Linda Casebeer** was born in Boone, Iowa, and over the years, has lived in the Midwest and South. Since taking a job at the University of Alabama at Birmingham, she and her husband have spent the past twenty-five years living in the Deep South, largely a mystery still to be explored. She is married to Edwin Casebeer, a writer and literature professor emeritus. They have five children. She met her husband at a long-running open mic poetry reading in a back room at the Alley Cat in Indianapolis, though the children often say they met in a bar.

Linda studied poetry first in community workshops led by Sean Farragher, supported by the South Carolina Arts

Commission. Later she studied for a year with Maura Stanton as a component of an English minor for her doctorate at Indiana University. Her poems have appeared in journals such as *Slant, Earth's Daughters, Chest, Hospital Drive, Pinyon, Crab Orchard Review, Canary, The Big Window Review, Bones, The Raven's Perch*. She has published one collection of poems, *The Last Eclipsed Moon*, from Cherry Grove Collections in 2008. She has worked as a medical education researcher investigating patterns of diffusion and adoption of innovations in medicine. What draws her to research and to poetry is the lyrical beauty of the unknown and the unknowable.

Made in USA - Kendallville, IN
1231649_9781952570612
02.11.2021 0822